The Value of CHARITY

The Story of Paul-Emile Léger

The Value of CHARITY

The Story of
Paul-Emile Léger

This is the story of a man who decided when
he was a little boy that he would dedicate
himself to others. He would let charity guide his
steps always. Some of the important events
of his life are described in the following pages.
A more complete biography will be found
on page 63.

Once upon a time...

not so very long ago, in the pretty village of Saint-Anicet, Quebec, there lived a dark-eyed little boy. His name was Paul-Emile Léger. Paul-Emile loved to climb the bell-tower of the village church. Perched up there, he could see all the way to the other side of Lake Saint-François. He could spend hours gazing across at the distant hills.

"Hello!" he would shout as loudly as he could.

"Hello! Hello!" the echo always answered.

One hot, dreamy day, Paul-Emile made a promise to himself. "Someday," he said, "I will go beyond those hills. In fact, I think I will go all around the world." And with that, he felt a gentle touch on his shoulder.

"Oh, Popol!" said Paul-Emile. "It's you."

"It's me all right," said Popol, "your guardian angel. Don't you think you've wasted enough time in daydreaming today?"

"I'm not day-dreaming," objected Paul-Emile indignantly. "I'm planning my future. You of all people should know that since you know my secret."

"Maybe so," answered the angel, "but you're forgetting that your father needs help in the store."

"You're right," said the boy. "Come on, let's go!"

Paul-Emile was glad he had Popol to remind him of his responsibilities.

He knew that guardian angels don't really talk to people. He knew that when he listened to Popol he was really listening to his own conscience. "Still," thought Paul-Emile, "since I started discussing things with Popol, I think I understand myself better."

Paul-Emile's father owned the village general store. It stood opposite the dock where supplies for the village were unloaded from big boats. Mr. Léger was a very strong man. He carried the heavy cases from the dock around to the back of the store. Paul-Emile's first job was to open them. Then he arranged the flour, eggs, sugar and molasses on the shelves. He was pleased and proud to be able to help his parents.

"When you grow up," Mr. Léger told his son one day, "all this will belong to you. It will be your store."

Paul-Emile didn't know quite what to say. He loved his father very much and didn't want to hurt him. "Thank you, Papa," he murmured, "but . . ."

Mr. Léger noticed that Paul-Emile was confused. He put an arm around his son's shoulders. "What's bothering you, son? Is there something you want to tell me?"

"When I grow up I want to be a priest," Paul-Emile finally blurted. "A missionary."

"That's a wonderful ambition," said his father. "But, you know, you must be very brave to become a missionary. You would have to leave your mother and me and your friends. You would have to live far away from your own country."

"I know that. But I read in a book that there are countries where lots of little children don't have any father or mother. Often they get sick because they have nothing to eat. I want to take them food and medicine and be their friend."

"Heaven have mercy on us," groaned Popol. "Where will these notions of Paul-Emile's end up leading us?"

In a quiet corner of the store, Paul-Emile scolded Popol. "Stop carrying on so, Popol," he said. "After all, you're the one who first told me about those poor little children. You told me that they don't know about the Baby Jesus. How can you expect me not to care what happens to them?"

"Of course I expect you to *care* about them," wailed Popol. "But do we have to take charity so far from home?" Seeing Paul-Emile's look of disapproval, he added, "Well, you know I've always been scared of unfamiliar things."

"Then you'd better start building up your courage right now," said Paul-Emile firmly. "My mind is made up. I am going to be a missionary."

Popol sighed. "I suppose I'll get used to the idea," he said. "It's going to be some time before you're old enough for us to leave."

Paul-Emile knew that it would not be easy to make his dream come true. He would have to prepare himself. He prayed to Jesus to help him and give him strength. Every morning he went to Mass with his grandmother. He loved his grandmother very much. No one was better at talking about Jesus than she was. After Mass, Paul-Emile would sit on the porch steps while his grandmother rocked in her chair. As they gazed at the sparkling waters of Lake Saint-François, he listened carefully to her every word.

"One day," she began, "God sent his son Jesus to Earth to bring us the Gospel."

"What's the Gospel, Grandma?" asked Paul-Emile.

"The word means 'good news,' my little one."

"Good news?"

"I'll explain. The 'good news' is the life of Jesus, told as a beautiful story to make us understand that all men on Earth are brothers. That's why we must love everyone, and especially those who are poor and unhappy and sick. We must do everything we can for them. That's called 'charity.'"

"I understand," said Paul-Emile. "One day I will carry the good news to little children all over the world."

Paul-Emile studied very hard at the village school. "A good missionary must be able to answer all the questions anyone asks," he reminded himself.

"True," remarked Popol, "but that's not all. You must learn to be a good speaker."

"What do you mean?" Paul-Emile asked him.

"You've got to learn to tell stories in an interesting way," explained Popol. "You can talk till you're blue in the face about charity and loving each other. If your talking puts people to sleep your words won't do them much good."

Paul-Emile thought this over. Finally he said, "The best story-teller I know is Tonton Masson."

The whole village of Saint-Anicet knew the stories of Tonton Masson, Paul-Emile's great-uncle. After supper, on long winter evenings, Tonton Masson and his friends would sit rocking around the wood stove in the center of the general store. People nicknamed them "the Nightwatchmen."

"Tonton," begged Paul-Emile, "tell the story about our ancestor, Luc-Hyacinthe Masson."

"Not again," groaned Popol, who knew it by heart.

"In those days, long ago," Tonton Masson began, "French Canadians were fighting the British. The French Canadians were called the *Patriotes*. They were only a handful of men and most of them didn't even have guns. Ah, but they were so brave! Their bravery astonished their enemies. For many days these few men held off the British. Alas, in the end, their battle was lost. Luc-Hyacinthe, your great-great-uncle

and my beloved father, fled to the woods. Later, he was captured and exiled to Bermuda. This all happened in 1837."

Tonton Masson always paused at this point in the story. For a few moments he smoked his pipe in silence. Finally, he continued: "After the war, my father came back home. His countrymen gave him a hero's welcome. He was elected to Parliament."

Although he had heard the story a hundred times, Paul-Emile listened spellbound to the very end.

"Tonton Masson is a great speaker," he told himself as he went up to bed. "I just hope that someday I can hold an audience that way with stories about the life of Jesus."

Paul-Emile's parents were proud of their son's decision to become a priest. They made up their minds that he should go to the best school possible.

The day came when Paul-Emile was to leave for the Seminary of Sainte-Thérèse. His father and mother took him to the railway station. When he heard the train whistle, Paul-Emile's heart sank. His mother wiped away a tear and gave him some last bits of advice.

"Be sure to work hard," she said. "You must learn Latin and Greek and mathematics. Be a good boy and don't forget your mother."

On the train, Paul-Emile felt very sad. He really wanted to go to the Seminary, but leaving home was hard. Popol racked his brain for a way to cheer up his friend. "Don't be sad, Paul-Emile," he said stifling a sob, "or I'll start crying too. Think of the children you will help someday. That should make you feel better."

Sadly, a great misfortune befell Paul-Emile soon after his arrival at the Seminary. He developed a nasty cough that simply wouldn't go away.

His teachers got very worried. "Poor little thing. He's wearing himself out. We'd better call the doctor."

The doctor came and examined Paul-Emile. "This boy is in a bad way," he said gravely. "I'm afraid his cough is an early sign of tuberculosis."

Tuberculosis is a very serious disease, and at that time it was quite common. The Father Superior thought that Paul-Emile should go back home.

"There, there now," said the Father Superior as he and Paul-Emile parted. "A good rest is all you need. Take care of yourself and come back to us soon."

Paul-Emile spent the rest of the school year at home. His mother spent many hours at his bedside. Little by little, he regained his strength, but he was very bored and depressed. His parents tried everything they could think of to distract him. One day, his father even suggested that he take apart the motor of the family car to help pass the time. Paul-Emile agreed, but quite clearly his heart wasn't in it.

"Popol," he asked over and over, "do you think I'll ever get to be a priest? I just can't believe that God could have any use for a weakling like me. Everything's ruined."

"God won't turn anybody away," Popol encouraged. "But instead of complaining all the time, why don't you apply yourself to something constructive?" The angel wanted to shake his friend out of his doldrums.

"But so far from the Seminary, what can I do?"

"For one thing, you can practice speaking before an audience. Have you forgotten the promise you made me? You promised that you would someday tell the story of Jesus' life. You promised to make it the most beautiful story anybody every heard."

So Paul-Emile got to work. Every day he rehearsed a little speech in front of his mirror. When he was satisfied with the results, he called his grandmother and his little brother, Jules, (Jules would one day become Govenor General of Canada.) and delivered his sermon to them.

"My dearest brothers," he would begin, imitating the parish priest. "Today I am going to talk to you about Christian charity. Do you ever give any thought to the little children who are starving to death in far-away countries? Jesus gave bread to those who had none. He consoled those who were sad. He nursed those who were ill."

Paul-Emile's grandmother had tears in her eyes when he had finished. She had never imagined that her own Paul-Emile would learn to speak so movingly.

That Christmas, during midnight Mass, something wonderful happened to Paul-Emile. The little church was filled with joyful organ music. The choir was singing "O Holy Night." Paul-Emile was deep in prayer. Suddenly he heard a voice say, very clearly, "You will be a priest."

"Did you hear that, Popol?" he whispered to his guardian angel on the way out of the church.

"Sure I did. And you owe me some thanks," answered Popol, bursting with pride. "I put in a word for you with my friends up there." Tapping his chest, he added, "I have influence in high places, you know."

Now that Paul-Emile was sure that his dream would come true, his health improved as if by magic. Soon he was back at school.

Although he had missed a year, he graduated with top honors. One of his teachers even gave him the unheard-of mark of 10½ out of 10.

"You remember all those evenings when you helped your classmates?" said Popol. "You could have been playing like the other boys. Instead you spent your time coaching boys who needed help. This success is your reward."

Paul-Emile rested that summer. In the autumn he began even more difficult studies at the Montreal Seminary. He worked without a break for four years.

At long last came the day of Paul-Emile's ordination, the day he would be made a priest. His family and all his friends gathered in the great cathedral in Montreal for the ceremony. As is the custom, Paul-Emile lay stretched on the floor at the Archbishop's feet to receive the sacrament. He felt that this was the most beautiful day of his whole life.

"At last I can say Mass," he murmured to Popol later.

"And preach . . . . Heaven knows, you've been practicing long enough!" Popol teased.

27

There was a fine reception after the ceremony. Popol couldn't sit still. He flitted from one guest to another, bowing deeply before the dignitaries. He kept coming back to Paul-Emile to make comments.

"Did you notice the Bishop's hat? Just look how high it is!"

"It's called a mitre, not a hat," Paul-Emile informed him.

"Do you know why a Bishop wears a hat?" asked Popol, ignoring the vocabulary lesson.

"Now what?" groaned Paul-Emile. He knew that Popol had dreamed up a joke and was bursting to tell it.

"It's because on the day he's made a Bishop the Holy Ghost descends onto his head. He quickly puts his hat on and keeps it on so the Holy Ghost can't get away."

A few years later, Paul-Emile's superiors felt he was ready to be a missionary. "We shall send him to Japan to found a seminary," they decided.

So Paul-Emile (who was now known to everyone as Father Léger) and his faithful companion, Popol, set off with some other missionaries on a big ship. The crossing took ten days. The sea was very rough, and many passengers were seasick. Nevertheless, Paul-Emile managed to say Mass every day. Sometimes, though, he had to balance himself as if he were walking a tightrope.

Early in the morning of the eleventh day he at last caught sight of the port of Yokohama, in Tokyo Bay.

"Come on, let's go stretch our legs," suggested one of the other missionaries after the boat docked. They had lots of time since the train that would take them to their final destination, Fukuoka, didn't leave till evening. They strolled along the streets of Tokyo, dodging rickshas—the two-wheeled passenger carts pulled by running men—and admiring the houses and the lanterns hanging in front of them.

"Everything's so crowded and so busy!" marvelled Paul-Emile. He was astonished at the speed with which bicyclists wove their way in and out among the rickshas.

Before they left Tokyo, the missionaries decided to have a typical Japanese meal in a restaurant.

Have you ever tried to eat rice with chopsticks? You arrange them between your thumb and fingers and pick food out of the dish with them. It takes practice. Father Léger had some trouble eating his bowl of rice. Watching him, Popol laughed till he hurt.

"Oh dear," he said when he caught his breath. "You really are the King of the Clumsies!"

"I'd like to see you do better!" replied Paul-Emile.

"Lucky for me angels don't have to eat," giggled Popol.

30

The train trip seemed endless. Nonetheless, Popol had only just settled down when the conductor announced "Fukuoka." It was a big city perched on a mountainside overlooking the sea.

The first important thing was to learn the language of the country. For six months Paul-Emile devoted all his time to studying Japanese. In the evening, his eyes red with tiredness, he dropped onto his *tatami*, the rice straw mat which the Japanese use for a bed.

"*O yasumi nasai*," called Popol, showing off.

"That's right. Goodnight, Popol."

At last the day came when Father Léger felt he spoke Japanese well enough to begin teaching about Jesus. He made his way through the bamboo forest and tall grass to a weather-beaten old building that looked about ready to fall down.

"*That's* your school?" exclaimed Popol.

They had no time to feel sorry for themselves, however, for the pupils had arrived. The children greeted their new teacher with ceremonious bows in the Japanese fashion.

"*Shimpu sama*," they all said together. That means "Honorable Father."

Father Léger was shown the way to his classroom, which was in the attic, and began his lesson.

"At last," he thought, "I am carrying the 'good news' to Japanese children."

One morning Paul-Emile found the school door bolted. A note was
pinned to it: "Closed because of cholera epidemic."

The whole city was in turmoil. Doctors worked day and night. Schools
and stores closed one after the other as the epidemic grew worse. Over
five hundred children under the age of six died in spite of the heroic
efforts of the emergency crews. "The poor little things," mourned
Popol.

Where do you think Father Léger was during the epidemic? Safe in his
room, hiding from the disease? Of course not. He too was working day
and night, nursing the sick. "Teaching about charity is important," he
thought as he sponged a sick baby's forehead. "But a good missionary
must always be ready to do whatever needs doing."

Everybody who saw how hard he worked for the sick children thought
he must be the most charitable man alive.

When the epidemic was over, everyone went back to his job. Paul-Emile returned to his young students. Carpenters meanwhile began to build the new seminary that would replace the old school.

Unfortunately, Father Léger would be obliged to leave Japan before his work was done. The Second World War was declared, and most of the countries in the world soon became involved. Japan and Canada found themselves on opposite sides. Officially, the Canadian missionaries were now enemies of Japan. But to the Japanese children they could never be anything but friends. As the priests said goodbye, the children were all in tears.

"Part of my heart will always be here in Japan," whispered Paul-Emile sadly to Popol.

Back in Canada, Paul-Emile did not remain idle. Everyone wanted to hear about his adventures in Japan. He began traveling from town to town to talk about his experiences. He dressed in a Japanese kimono and wore a long beard. He told his stories with such feeling that more than a few listeners started dreaming of becoming missionaries.

His superiors were so pleased with his work that they put Paul-Emile in charge of the parish of Valleyfield, the town where he had been born. His parents wasted no time in moving back to Valleyfield. They found a house right next door to his residence. What a joy it was for them to live near their eldest son again after such a long separation!

As soon as the war was over, our traveler set off again. This time he was sent to Rome. He would be in charge of a college for young Canadian priests.

"What desolation!" he sighed as he crossed Italy. The war had left the country in ruins. Houses had been gutted, boats sunk, docks smashed. And on the roadside were children in rags, begging passers-by, "Food. Give us food, please."

"Roll up your sleeves, Popol," announced Paul-Emile. "We're going to help all these poor victims of the war."

"But how?" objected Popol. "There are so many, and we have no money."

But to someone with a deep sense of charity, obstacles do not exist.

"I have an idea!" exclaimed Paul-Emile, after thinking for a few minutes. "I'll write to our friends in Canada. When I explain the terrible conditions under which the Italians are living, they will want to help."

"If you write as well as you preach," agreed Popol, "we have nothing to worry about. We'll get enough to feed the world."

Popol was right. A few weeks after he wrote his letters, Paul-Emile went to the railway station in Rome to collect five box-car loads of supplies. Jam, corn syrup, cod liver oil, medicine . . . there was everything.

"Have these crates taken to the Pope's storehouse," he ordered.

Everyone in Rome knew that Pope Pius XII was gathering donations of provisions from around the world. He then distributed the food and clothing to needy Italians. When he saw so many crates arrive at once, he was astonished.

"Where do all these packages come from?" asked the Holy Father.

"From Canada, Your Holiness," explained Paul-Emile. "I sent out an appeal in your name, and my friends responded generously.

"Come here, my son," said Pius XII. "Come here so I can bless you."

It was the beginning of a deep friendship between the Pope and the Canadian priest, who now became Monsignor Léger. Every month more crates of food arrived from Canada. The Pope couldn't praise his new friend enough. Newspapers printed stories about the exploits of Paul-Emile and the affection in which the Pope held him.

Every Canadian who passed through Rome had a favor to ask of Monsignor Léger. "Since you are such a friend of the Pope's, can you get me an audience with him?"

Paul-Emile obliged. He was always welcome in the Pope's personal quarters—a very rare privilege.

Pope Pius XII enjoyed Paul-Emile's company. (He also loved the fudge that Mrs. Léger sent to him through her son!) Nonetheless, the day came when he had to send his young friend away. He had a more important mission for him.

Do you know where he sent Paul-Emile?

He sent him to Montreal to become Archbishop. When Popol heard the news, he fainted.

"Oh boy! Missionary, parish priest, now Archbishop! What next? Just so long as you don't let all these honors go to your head!"

Popol need not have worried. Of course, the honors pleased Paul-Emile. But what he really cared about was the opportunity his new position would give him to help still more people.

Leaving Popol to cope with his astonishment, Paul-Emile packed his bags. Then he went to the Vatican to take his leave of the Pope. Pius XII embraced him for a moment and said, "I am very sad to see you go, Monsignor Léger."

The bells of all the churches in Montreal rang to greet Paul-Emile on his return. Popol couldn't get over it.

"When I think that you have a throne and vestments embroidered with gold thread and jewels worthy of a king!" he exclaimed, overwhelmed by so much magnificence.

Paul-Emile let him rave on. He knew that the task the Pope had entrusted to him was a difficult one. Montreal had many poor families that suffered from cold and hunger. Already there were hundreds of letters piled up on his desk. He opened the biggest envelope. On a piece of white paper, someone had drawn a foot. Underneath the drawing was written, "I am eight years old and I have no shoes. I've traced my foot so that you can get me a pair of shoes. Thank you. Marie-Josée."

Of course, Marie-Josée got a fine new pair of shoes the very next day.

Paul-Emile made a solemn promise to Montrealers. "As long as there are poor people in Montreal, I will not take a single day of rest."

And he kept his promise. From that day on, the poor from all corners of Montreal came knocking at his door.

"Help me," begged one. "I have a family of five to feed and I can't find work."

"I'm paralyzed from the waist down," cried another. "I have no family, no one at all to help me."

One morning someone left a four-month-old baby in a wicker basket on the cathedral steps. The baby was deaf, mute and blind. A band around his tiny wrist read only "Walter."

"Poor Walter," sighed Paul-Emile as he picked him up. "So small and so helpless. One more who's looking for a family."

Popol was pacing up and down, shaking his head in frustration.

"You listen to me, Paul-Emile," he finally exploded. "There are so many people without homes. What if we created a great big famliy that could take them all in?"

"That's a wonderful idea!" exclaimed Paul-Emile. "We'll start by building a house. It will be big and cheerful and warm."

He phoned a carpenter he knew. The carpenter knew a plumber, who knew an electrician, whose son was a plasterer.

"Bring along your relatives and friends," he suggested to everybody. "There's lots of work."

Together they built a long house of red brick. "We'll call it 'Charity House,'" Archbishop Léger proudly announced, putting away his tools after a long day's work.

No sooner was the work finished than the house was full. Everyone who came to live there became part of a large, happy family. The ones who could walk ran errands for those who were paralyzed. The ones who could see read to the blind. Everyone seemed very happy.

But one morning Popol noticed a worried look on Paul-Emile's face. "Oh, oh, that's a bad sign," he said to himself. "What's the trouble now?"

"Popol," explained Paul-Emile, "it's almost Christmas and we don't have a cent in the bank. And the people of the city have been so generous, we really can't ask them for more."

He sank wearily into a chair. "I would so have liked to provide a good Christmas for our residents."

"Just leave it to me," advised Popol reassuringly. "I'll take care of it. Angel's honor!"

Can you guess what happened?

On Christmas Eve, just before midnight, a truck pulled up to the kitchen door.
"I've been told to deliver these cases here," said the driver.

"But who sent you?" asked Archbishop Léger.

"There was no name given," replied the driver as he left.

What treats awaited the residents of Charity House! Stuffed turkey with cranberry sauce, hot rolls, cakes, pies, ice cream. There were Christmas stockings filled with oranges and candies. The mysterious benefactor had even remembered garlands and bells and tinsel to decorate the dining room. After midnight Mass everyone sat down for the feast. And Walter, who had won everyone's heart, was seated right next to Archbishop Léger at the head table.

In Rome, Pope Pius XII heard of Archbishop Léger's charitable works.

"I shall make him a Cardinal," he announced.

Do you know what a Cardinal is?

A Cardinal is a prince of the Church. To be made a Cardinal is a great honor indeed. Cardinals come from every country in the world. They are the Pope's principal advisors. When the Pope dies, the Cardinals choose the new Pope from among themselves. This is the supreme honor.

Archbishop Léger traveled to Rome where the Pope placed the *biretta*—a red hat reserved for Cardinals—on his head. When he returned to Canada, the proud Montrealers had decorated all the streets. Never before had the city seen such a display. Flags waved in the wind and banners fluttered from the snow-covered trees. Artists had even carved wonderful sculptures in ice.

"Long live our Cardinal!" cried the people lining the streets. "Long live our Prince!"

Mounted policemen cleared the way for the car bearing the new Cardinal. Paul-Emile was dressed all in red. As the procession moved slowly along the streets, the crowd knelt on either side to receive their Prince's blessing.

All over the city, religious ceremonies and banquets were held day after day. And when all the celebrations finally ended, what do you think Paul-Emile did? Perhaps he felt he could rest on his laurels?

Not Paul-Emile! He worked harder than ever. He founded an orphanage, a hospital for people with incurable illnesses and a home for the aged. "We'll call it 'Heaven's Gate'," he decided.

A few years later, a great sorrow came to Paul-Emile. Pope Pius XII died at the age of eighty-two.

"I have lost a friend," he sadly told Popol. "More than a friend, a father."

The day after he heard the sad news, Paul-Emile flew to Rome. There he met other Cardinals from all over the world, and they gathered together in the Sistine Chapel to choose a new Pope. Each Cardinal wrote on a piece of paper the name of his choice for the next Pope.

A huge crowd was gathered outside waiting for the Cardinals to decide. Suddenly a cloud of white smoke appeared in the sky above the chapel. This was the signal the people were waiting for. It meant that a new Pope had been chosen. A great shout went up. "*Viva il papa!*" "Long live the Pope!"

It was a deeply moved Paul-Emile who emerged from the chapel. "I am sure," he murmured to Popol, "that John XXIII will be an extraordinary Pope."

For the next ten years, Cardinal Léger continued his work among the poor and the sick of Montreal. Then, one day, he made an announcement that stunned the country.

Only Popol was not taken by surprise. Paul-Emile had, of course, already told his faithful companion his plans.

"Popol, get your things ready. We're leaving."

Popol couldn't believe his ears. "Leaving? But where for?"

"I want to be a missionary again," replied Paul-Emile.

"You can't be serious!" Popol exclaimed. "There's still so much to do here. You're not going to abandon the poor unfortunates of your own city!"

"I won't be abandoning them. Our devoted helpers will carry on our work. And you and I are going to a country where there is a thousand times more misery than there is here."

"We're going back to Japan? Poor you! To think you'll have to eat your rice with chopsticks again and take your bath in an enormous tub of boiling hot water!" Popol giggled.

"No, Popol, this time we're going to Africa, to Cameroun."

"Is it nice there?"

"It's a beautiful country. But thousands upon thousands of people there suffer from hunger and leprosy."

"'Leprosy'? What's that?"

"It's a terrible disease, and it's contagious—that is, it spreads from one person to another. Many poor people get it. Those who have it badly get spots all over their body. They can end up losing their hands or feet."

The people of Montreal cried as they watched their Cardinal climb on the plane. But, sad as they were, they knew that he was a great man. They recognized that it was charity which led him to leave his city to go work among the lepers.

"Here, take this money," said a spokesman, pressing a thick envelope into Paul-Emile's hands. "When you build your hospitals for lepers, think of us."

Paul-Emile was barely able to hold back the tears as he disappeared into the plane. Popol cleared his throat and murmured, "At least it's not just bad things like diseases that are contagious. Good things like charity can be as well."

After hours and hours in the air, the plane began its descent into Yaoundé, the city of seven hills, capital of Cameroun. Paul-Emile gazed in wonder at the rice paddies and banana plantations surrounding the city.

"This is the heart of Africa," he told Popol.

How different would be the life that awaited him here! No more palatial home like the one he'd had in Montreal. From now on he would be living in a trailer in the bush. No more rich red robes either. In Africa, missionaries wore long white robes.

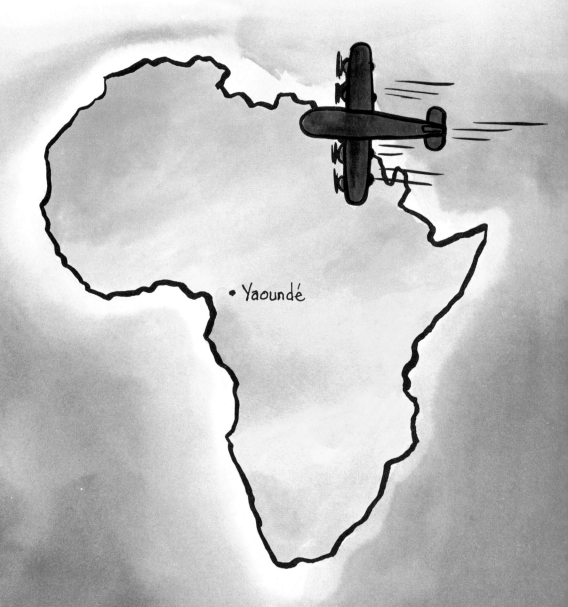

Every day the Cardinal made a tour of the hospitals, called leprosariums, that were being built under his supervision. One morning, as he was about to leave his trailer, he noticed a small, shrivelled boy near the door. As soon as the child caught sight of Paul-Emile, he turned and began to drag himself painfully away through the dust.

"What's your name, child?" asked Paul-Emile, catching up to him easily.

"Good-for-Nothing," answered the boy. "Sometimes they call me 'Snake-Boy' because I have to drag myself instead of walking. My legs are dead."

"Don't you go to school?" asked the Cardinal.

"No. Children who don't walk aren't allowed in schools here."

"Well, I'll make you a promise, little Good-for-Nothing. Soon you shall go to school, just like children everywhere in the world."

"I get the feeling that Paul-Emile is cooking up some new project," observed Popol, as he watched the scene.

Wanting to know more, he jumped into the jeep beside Paul-Emile, who was just setting off.

"Well?" he demanded.

"It seems to me that if these handicapped children received medical attention, some of them at least might get better. But the government is going to have to help me in this project."

Before long he was explaining his plan to the country's president, Ahmadou Ahidjo. "I would like to found a center for the care and treatment of handicapped children," he told him.

The president thought this was an excellent idea. "I will give you all the help I can," he promised.

African workers built a long, low house. It was very bright and airy, surrounded by a garden of feathery, scented mimosa trees. When it was ready, Paul-Emile hired doctors and nurses.

Good-for-Nothing became the center's first patient. The doctors fitted him with leg-braces which allowed him to stand upright.

"I didn't know I was so tall!" exclaimed the little boy.

Paul Emile hadn't forgotten his promise to Good-for-Nothing. He hired an African teacher for the center. The teacher gave lessons in reading, writing and arithmetic to all the children.

At the same time, Good-for-Nothing was working very hard at learning how to use his legs again. A nurse taught him some exercises to strengthen his muscles. Before long he was able to take a few steps.

"See how well I walk?" he said to the Cardinal one day.

"Yes, you're much better, Good-for-Nothing. So much better that you can go home now and attend the village school."

"But I'll be so sad to leave you."

"I'll be sad too, Good-for-Nothing. But we must think of all the other handicapped children who are waiting for a place in the center so that they can be helped too."

So Good-for-Nothing prepared himself to leave. First, though, he asked a favor of Cardinal Léger.

"Would you baptize me?"

"Yes, of course," answered the Cardinal. "Have you chosen a name for yourself? You can't be called Good-for-Nothing anymore."

The little boy nodded. "I'd like to be called Paul-Emile."

After the baptism, Popol went to shake hands with the new Paul-Emile's guardian angel.

"I guess they'll be calling you Popol too now," he remarked, beaming.

It was getting late. The young Paul-Emile would have to leave if he was to be home by nightfall. Cardinal Léger watched him as he made his way slowly across the reddish earth, proud of the new-found strength in his legs.

"Don't forget your promise," the Cardinal called after him.

"I'll never forget it," called back the former Good-for-Nothing, now Paul-Emile. "Every night before I go to sleep I'll ask myself, 'Have I done something for someone today?'"

Like Good-for-Nothing, hundreds of handicapped children learned to walk at the center. Others learned to use wheelchairs and crutches. Not all handicapped people can be cured. But if someone cares enough to help them, they can all learn to develop the abilities they have.

The whole world was proud of Cardinal Léger's center for the re-education of the handicapped. Naturally Cameroun was grateful to him. He was named a Commander of the Order of Value and Merit of the Republic of Cameroun. He was awarded the Lester B. Pearson medal by the United Nations Association in Canada. This award is given to people who have worked very hard for peace.

Paul-Emile was pleased to receive these honors, of course. His greatest joy, however, was to see the little handicapped children cared for and sometimes cured.

Not all of us will become missionaries. We will not all devote our lives to helping the unfortunate as Paul-Emile did. But we all know people who are lonely and need a smile, handicapped people who need help, or unfortunate people who need love. And we can all try our best to do something for such people. That, too, is charity.

Practicing charity brought Paul-Emile Léger a great deal of happiness. Perhaps you might like to think about the possible joys that helping others could hold for you.

The End

PAUL-EMILE LEGER
1904-

Paul-Emile Léger was born in Valleyfield in southwestern Quebec on April 25, 1904. He was the eldest of two children. (His brother, Jules, would one day become Canada's twenty-first Governor-General.) Shortly after his birth, his parents moved to Saint-Anicet, some thirty kilometres away, where his father ran the general store.

After school, Paul-Emile helped his father in the store. In the evening, he would sit on the stairs and listen to the old-timers of the village tell stories as they rocked and smoked their pipe around the wood stove.

His maternal grandmother sparked his interest in religion. They would sit together while she explained in simple words the mysteries of the Catholic faith. These moments and her words remained engraved in Paul-Emile's memory.

At the age of twelve Paul-Emile went to study at the Sainte-Thérèse Seminary, a long train ride from his home. Illness, however, soon forced him to leave the school. It took him a year to recover, and he despaired of ever fulfilling his dream of becoming a missionary. But while he was at midnight Mass on Christmas Eve that year, he heard a voice which told him, "You will be a priest."

After regaining his health, Paul-Emile finished his classical studies and began a four-year course in theology at the Grand Séminaire de Montréal. On May 25, 1929, he was ordained a priest in the Sulpician order. He then went to Paris to study canon law (the laws of the Catholic Church) and taught at the seminary of Issy-les-Moulineaux.

In 1933 his dream finally came true: he was sent as a missionary to Fukuoka, Japan. Within six months he had learned enough Japanese to teach catechism and preach in that language. He founded a seminary, but was obliged to return to Canada when the Second World War broke out.

Back in Canada, Father Léger was put in charge of the parish of Valleyfield. Over the next few years he built up a reputation as a brilliant and persuasive speaker. Then, on the last Sunday in April 1947, he broke the news to his parishioners that he was leaving them. He was going to Italy to become rector of the Canadian College, an establishment for young Canadian priests studying in Rome. In addition to his duties as rector, he undertook those of Canadian ambassador to the Vatican.

Italy was in ruins in the aftermath of the war. Everywhere children in rags begged for food. Paul-Emile could not bear the sight of so much suffering. He launched an appeal for help, and Canadians responded generously with food, clothing and medicine. His efforts greatly moved Pope Pius XII and a deep friendship developed between them.

In 1950 Pius XII appointed Paul-Emile Archbishop of Montreal. From the moment he assumed his new duties, Paul-Emile spared no effort in his fight against poverty. He founded Charity House, a home for the chronically ill, and Saint-Charles Borromée Hospital for old men who were sick and had no family. Later he concerned himself with the problems of juvenile delinquents, old women and orphans. He organized work parties of volunteers to construct and repair buildings which then became hostels for the underprivileged.

On January 12, 1953, Pope Pius XII elevated Archbishop Léger to the rank of Cardinal. Montrealers were so proud to have one of their own become the youngest Cardinal of his day that they decorated the city in his honor as it had never been decorated before.

After eighteen years of devoted work in Montreal the "Cardinal of the poor" left the city to become a missionary again. He had decided to do something for the lepers of Africa and set out for Cameroun. Over the next few years he founded and helped finance the construction of 82 leprosariums. But his most important work was the founding of a center for the rehabilitation of handicapped children in Yaoundé, the capital of Cameroun. From far and near, parents brought their polio-stricken children to the center, where they received medical care, physiotherapy and schooling.

Living in a modest trailer nearby, Cardinal Léger watched over his little proteges and launched a polio-prevention campaign.

In 1979, Paul-Emile Léger returned to settle permanently in Montreal, where he spends much of his time raising funds for charitable works in Third World countries. Every year he goes back to spend a few weeks in Africa where a part of his heart always remains.

The ValueTale Series